FAITH
SERIES

Study Guide

KENNETH
COPELAND

FAITH
SERIES

Study Guide

KENNETH COPELAND

KENNETH
COPELAND
PUBLICATIONS

Faith Series

ISBN-10 1-57562-670-5   30-0721
ISBN-13 978-1-57562-670-3

21 20 19 18 17 16   10 9 8 7 6 5

Kenneth Copeland Publications
Fort Worth, TX 76192-0001

For more information about Kenneth Copeland Ministries, visit kcm.org or call 1-800-600-7395 (U.S. only) or +1-817-852-6000.

1

> "...*And this is the victory that overcometh the world, even our faith.*"

1 John 5:4

Real Bible faith makes you an overcomer.
Real Bible faith always says what the Word says.

CD ONE
Real Bible Faith

"For whatsoever is born of God overcometh the world: and this is the victory that overcometh the world, even our faith. Who is he that overcometh the world, but he that believeth that Jesus is the Son of God?"

1 John 5:4-5

You have the right to overcome if you are born of God. You are born of God if you believe that Jesus is the Christ. Use your victory that comes from God—your faith—to overcome in every situation.

Act on God's Word by Faith
and Live Fear-Free

FOCUS: "So then faith cometh by hearing, and hearing by the word of God" (Romans 10:17).

Where does faith come from?

God is the Father of faith, and from the beginning, He intended for His children to live by faith. Since God was Adam's spiritual Father before the Fall, Adam lived by faith. But when Adam fell, his spiritual father became Satan, the father of fear. Fear replaced Adam's faith, and it became necessary for God to send Jesus to redeem man in order to restore him to the state he was in before the Fall.

Living by faith is a way of life for God's people.

Jesus was made a curse for you (Galatians 3:13-14). If you have accepted Him as Lord, you are redeemed from the curse of the law. You are no longer bound by anything listed under the curse in Deuteronomy 28.

You can go to the Word and find out how to exercise that redemption in your life. Romans 10:17 says that faith comes from hearing the Word of God. As John 8:32 says, "Ye shall know the truth, and the truth shall make you free." Knowing the Word and acting on it in faith will give you control of the situations you are facing. It will also make you free from any fear the enemy tries to bring.

Fear has no place in the life of a believer. Faith should always be the lifestyle of God's people. Galatians 3:11 says, "The just shall live by faith."

Real Bible faith always wants to know what the Word says. *It's God's will in every situation.* Matthew 6:10 says, "Thy will be done in earth, as it is in heaven." Philippians 4:19 goes on to say, "But my God shall supply all your need according to his riches in glory by

Christ Jesus." Obviously, heaven is a total manifestation of God's will. According to Matthew 6:10, having all your needs supplied is also God's will for you here on earth.

God has provided the meeting of your needs through Jesus Christ. Go to the Word of God, find out what His will is in your situation and start believing for it. The Bible is a revelation of the love of God and what He *will* do for you.

Even under the old covenant, God was doing everything He could to get His Word into the hands of people so they would act on it. He told His people that in order to live in victory, they would have to walk on His Word by faith (Joshua 1:7-8).

If you are a Christian, start saying what Jesus would say and acting as He would act in every situation. Keep the Word in your mouth and in your actions. Become committed to the Lord and become committed to the Word of God. You'll start bearing the kind of fruit that will glorify God. As Matthew 7:16 says, "Ye shall know them by their fruits...."

Trust the One Who Always Finishes What He Starts Concerning You

FOCUS: "Looking unto Jesus the author and finisher of our faith..." (Hebrews 12:2).

The strength of your faith will be in direct proportion to the amount of the Word of God that is fed into it. Faith comes by *hearing the Word.*

Hebrews 12:2 says, "Looking unto Jesus the author and finisher of our faith...." How do you look unto Jesus? By looking to the Word. Jesus and the Word are one. Looking unto Jesus is looking into and acting on the Word, not the circumstances. The moment you act on the Word, Jesus is instantly involved.

Believing is acting. If you believe it, you will act on it. If there is no action, there is no faith. "Even so faith, if it hath not works [corresponding actions], is dead, being alone" (James 2:17). Faith is more than accepting what you hear, see or feel. It is believing enough to act on it.

Become a doer of the Word and not a hearer only. The Apostle James said if we are hearers only, we are self-deceived (James 1:22). In Luke 6:46, Jesus says, "And why call ye me, Lord, Lord, and do not the things which I say?" In other words, He is saying, "Why do you deceive yourself and call Me Lord when you don't let Me reign in your life by letting the Word be first place?" If the Word is not final authority, then Jesus is not in a position of lordship in your life.

It's like the man who built his house on the sand. He was deceived. He could not stand against the forces of this world without a foundation.

The Word is the source of our faith. Faith was given to us so we can enforce Satan's defeat in our lives...and live in victory.

Now Begin Enjoying It

Get in the Word of God and find out what He thinks about your situation. Take His thoughts and His precepts from the Word and believe that instead of natural circumstances. Then act on it. It will cause Jesus to be involved with you vitally and He will become real to you.

Remember, as a believer you are an overcomer, and this is the victory that overcomes the world...*even your faith.*

CD 1 Outlined

I. God's Word is His will
A. Knowing God's will is essential to receiving from Him
B. The Bible is a revelation of the love of God

II. Christ has redeemed us from the curse of the law (Galatians 3:13-14)
A. Go to the Word and find out how to exercise that redemption in your life
B. "And ye shall know the truth, and the truth shall make you free" (John 8:32)

III. Jesus is the author and finisher, or developer, of your faith (Hebrews 12:2)
A. The strength of your faith is in direct proportion to the amount of Word fed into it
B. Jesus and the Word are one

IV. If you believe, you will act
A. If there is no action, there is no faith
B. Faith without works [corresponding action] is dead (James 2:17)

V. The foundation of Christians' faith is the Word
A. Living by faith is a way of life for God's people (Galatians 3:11)
B. The Word is the source of our faith
C. The victory that overcomes the world is our faith

Study Questions

(1) How can a believer overcome the things of the world? _____

_____

_____

_____

(2) Where does faith come from? _____

_____

_____

_____

(3) Who is the author and finisher of our faith? _____

_____

_____

_____

_____

(4) Explain the difference between accepting what you hear, see or feel,
and faith. _____

_____

_____

_____

(5) Why are we deceived when we call Jesus, Lord, and are not doing
the Word? _____

_____

_____

_____

Study Notes

"If ye abide in me, and my words abide in you,
ye shall ask what ye will, and it shall be done unto you."
John 15:7

"...*And Jesus answering saith
unto them, Have
faith in God* [*Have the
God kind of faith*]."

Mark 11:22

Jesus said we can have faith like God has.
In fact, that's how we should be living...every day.

CD TWO
Application of the God Kind of Faith

If You Have the God Kind of Faith, It Will Be in Two Places—In Your Mouth and in Your Heart

"*T*he word is nigh thee, even in thy mouth, and in thy heart: that is, the word of faith, which we preach."
Romans 10:8

Living by God's Kind of Faith—It's a Way of Life for God's People

FOCUS: "The just shall live by faith" (Romans 1:17).

The application of faith is not by chance or by accident. It is a decision. It is a way of life for God's people, and the Word tells us how to do it.

Faith is a spiritual law. It is set forth in Jesus' teaching in Mark 11:23-24. In this passage, Jesus was teaching on powerful faith—the kind of faith that will move and change things. He was talking about the *God kind of faith*.

In Romans 10:8, the Apostle Paul said, "The word is nigh thee, even in thy mouth, and in thy heart: that is, the word of faith, which we preach." If you have the God kind of faith, it will be in two places—in your mouth and in your heart. Both Paul and Jesus are describing God's method of operation—using the mouth to release faith—saying and believing.

Christians receive all the promises of God by faith. But if faith does not seem to be working in a given situation, there is a need to find out from God's Word how to put it to work. The Word is the believer's spiritual manual to a faith-filled life.

When you find out what God thinks about a situation, it will change your thinking. Psalm 119:130 says, "The entrance of thy words giveth light...." Once a man finds a truth from the Word of God, and he gets light on that situation, then he can exercise his faith on it. He can walk in the light of what he has found, and it will begin to produce in his life.

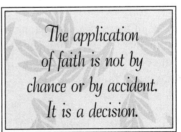

The application of faith is not by chance or by accident. It is a decision.

"So then faith cometh by hearing, and hearing by the word of

God" (Romans 10:17). The Word produces faith. But your faith will never exceed your knowledge of the Word. As you gain this knowledge, your thinking will conform to what the Word says. Your thoughts will be in line with God's thoughts. The Holy Spirit will take the Word and teach you all things. He will guide you into all truth.

In addition, your faith will not work above the level of your confession. So keep confessing the Word. Hebrews 4:12, 14 says: "For the word of God is quick [alive], and powerful, and sharper than any twoedged sword, piercing even to the dividing asunder of soul and spirit, and of the joints and marrow, and is a discerner of the thoughts and intents of the heart.... Seeing then that we have a great high priest, that is passed into the heavens, Jesus the Son of God, let us hold fast our profession."

God has provided His Word and Jesus' high priestly ministry. The only thing He told us to do is to hold fast to our profession, or our confession. We already saw that Jesus said you can have what you say. So what have you been saying with your mouth?

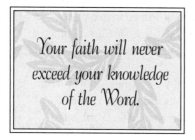

Your faith will never exceed your knowledge of the Word.

Matthew 12:34 says, "Out of the abundance of the heart the mouth speaketh." What's in your heart in abundance? It's going to be whatever you have been feeding on. Whether it's television or the Word of God, what you have been giving attention to is what will come out of your mouth.

Proverbs 18:21 says, "Death and life are in the power of the tongue: and they that love it shall eat the fruit thereof." Start filling your heart with the Word, and let that be what comes out of your mouth. Begin to live like God does...by the God kind of faith.◄❧

Now Begin Enjoying It

The following four steps are the *Application Formula for the God Kind of Faith:*

1. Say it. Faith is released with the mouth. When God created the universe,

He used words. When He spoke, things happened. In His earthly ministry, Jesus spoke words of life to the sick and diseased, and they were made whole. As believers, we can take what the Word says and speak it with confidence. We are not speaking from our own ability but from the power of God that resides within us.

2. *Do it.* Act on the Word. Faith without corresponding action is dead (James 2:17). Take what God says as you would take the word of a trusted friend. God's Word is His bond — it will never fail (Matthew 24:35).

3. *Receive it.* When you pray, believe you receive that which you desire. The answer is already a fact in the spiritual realm, but your faith brings it into the physical realm.

4. *Tell it.* Do not wait until you see the answer; testify that it is yours according to the Word. Give God praise and thanksgiving for what He has done in your life.

God's Word works every time, but we must apply our faith to that Word before we see the manifestation. Signs follow the believer. Signs follow faith in God's Word. It's time to start living every day by faith…the God kind of faith.

CD 2 Outlined

I. Applying faith is a decision and a way of life for God's people
    A. Jesus said, "Have the God kind of faith" (Mark 11:22)
    B. "The just shall live by faith" (Romans 1:17)

II. Faith is a spiritual law
    A. The law of faith is set forth in Mark 11:22-26
    B. The word of faith is in your mouth and heart (Romans 10:8)

III. God's Word produces faith
    A. Faith comes by hearing the Word (Romans 10:17)
    B. Your faith will never exceed your knowledge of the Word
    C. The Holy Spirit uses the Word to teach and guide you

IV. Your faith will not work above the level of your confession
    A. The Word is alive and powerful
    B. Jesus is the High Priest of your confession
    C. Hold fast your confession (Hebrews 4:12-14)

V. Application formula for the God kind of faith
    A. Say it: Speak the Word
    B. Do it: Act on the Word
    C. Receive it: Believe you receive when you pray
    D. Tell it: Testify that it's yours. Praise and thank God that it's done

Study Questions

(1) Where is the law of faith set forth in the Bible? _____

_____

_____

_____

_____

(2) What determines the amount of faith that we have operating in our lives? _____

_____

_____

_____

_____

(3) List the four steps for the application of the God kind of faith. _____

_____

_____

_____

_____

_____

(4) Give a brief statement of explanation about each step. _____

_____

_____

_____

_____

_____

Study Notes

"For with the heart man believeth unto righteousness;
and with the mouth confession is made unto salvation."
Romans 10:10

3

"We having the same
spirit of faith, according
as it is written, I believed, and
therefore have I
spoken; we also believe,
and therefore speak."

2 Corinthians 4:13

If you believe—if you have faith, then you will speak.
That's how you release your faith.

CD THREE
Releasing the Power of Faith

"*And* Jesus answering saith unto them,

Have faith in God. For verily I say unto you,

That whosoever shall say unto this mountain,

Be thou removed, and be thou cast into the sea;

and shall not doubt in his heart, but shall believe

that those things which he saith shall come to

pass; he shall have whatsoever he saith."

Mark 11:22-23

Receive From God on Purpose by Releasing the Power of Faith Through Your Words

FOCUS: "[Have the faith of God]...whosoever shall say unto this mountain...and shall not doubt in his heart, but shall believe...he shall have whatsoever he saith" (Mark 11:22-23).

"The word is nigh thee, even in thy mouth, and in thy heart: that is, the word of faith.... For with the heart man believeth unto righteousness; and with the mouth confession is made unto salvation" (Romans 10:8, 10).

Out of the spirit of man come the forces of life, including the force of faith. That's why Proverbs 4:23 says, "Keep thy heart with all diligence; for out of it are the issues of life." Galatians 5:22 calls these issues, or forces, the fruit of the spirit. Each one of them can be released on purpose, but the force of faith is the primary one that brings results. It is also the force that is primary in pleasing God (Hebrews 11:6). In this lesson, we will study how to release this powerful force.

As believers, we must learn to have confidence in our faith in order to live a victorious life. It is the faith of God in us that releases the power of God to bring our words to pass. We must believe that when we speak, what we say will come to pass. Mark 11:23 says: "...but shall believe that those things which he saith shall come to pass." Not just a few, but all the words we speak will come to pass.

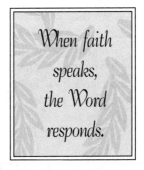

When faith speaks, the Word responds.

In Mark 11:22-24, Jesus outlined how to use the faith of God—by saying and believing—by using faith-filled words. Paul said, "As it is written, I believed, and therefore have I spoken; we also believe, and therefore speak" (2 Corinthians 4:13). Your faith is released by the words of your mouth.

Hebrews 3:1 says that Jesus is the Apostle and High Priest of our profession, or confession. As High Priest, He is our mouthpiece, our lawyer. He pleads our case to the Father. First John 2:1 says that if we sin, we have an advocate with the Father, Jesus Christ.

But He is also the Apostle of our profession. The word translated *apostle* means a "sent one." He is sent to see to it that our confession is carried out. As we speak God's Word in faith, He is watching over that Word to perform it in our lives.

Jesus is the Word of God. God sent His Word to meet every need of mankind, and the Word will produce the manifestation of the answer to that need. When faith speaks, the Word responds.

There Are Four Classifications of Confessions Taught in the New Testament

1. Confession of sin under the old covenant: Under the old covenant, to *repent* meant "to be sorry for" your sin, for breaking the covenant of God.

2. Confession of the sinner today: Today the unborn-again man is to confess the lordship of Jesus.

3. Confession of sin by the believer: Ask the Lord to forgive you when you miss it. First John 2:1 says, "If any man sin, we have an advocate with the Father, Jesus Christ the righteous." Romans 8:1 says, "There is therefore now no condemnation to them which are in Christ Jesus...."

4. Confession of faith in the Word, in Christ and in God the Father: Say what the Word says about you. God's Word will not return unto Him void (Isaiah 55:11). Return the Word to Him in prayer...as the voice of your confession. Whatever you receive from God, confession is made unto it.

As Believers, What Are We to Confess?

We must confess what God, in Christ, has wrought for *us in the plan of redemption.* Any time we see in the Bible the phrases "in Him," "in whom," "in Christ," it is speaking about us personally because of what Jesus did for us on the cross. It does not pertain to what we were. It is what we are now.

Confess what God, through the Word, by the Holy Spirit, is doing in you. When you find out who you are and confess it, in faith, then the Holy Spirit will take that Word and build an awareness of it on the inside of you. The Word becomes a reality. The Holy Spirit reveals the truth to you.

Confess what you are to *God in Christ.* You are a child of the King, a joint heir with Jesus. He sees you according to what the Word says you are—righteous, victorious, seated with Him in heavenly places, healed and prosperous. Take your rightful place and rule over your circumstances.

Confess what Jesus is doing for you now *at the right hand of the Father.* Continually confess Jesus is Lord. Confess Him as Lord over your body, Lord over your finances and Lord over every other area of your life. His throne is forever. As the King of kings, He is Lord over all. God put all things under His feet and gave Him to be the Head over all things to the Church.

Confess what God, by His Word, can do through us. God uses people. The believer is God's representative here on earth. With His Word on our lips, we can do even greater works than Jesus did in His earthly ministry. We can bring others into the saving knowledge of the truth. We can give forth the healing message. We can see people set free and delivered by the words of life we speak. ᴄᴗ

CD 3 Outlined

I. You can receive from God on purpose by releasing the power of faith
   A. Faith is released through faith-filled words
   B. Say, believe, have what you say (Mark 11:22-23)
   C. Issues, or forces, of life come out of the spirit of man (Proverbs 4:23)
   D. It is God's faith in you that releases the power
   E. Believe all you say will come to pass

II. Jesus is the Apostle and High Priest of our profession (Hebrews 3:1)
   A. Apostle
      1. Sent One
      2. He is sent to see that our confession is carried out
   B. High Priest
      1. Advocate, mouthpiece, lawyer
      2. He pleads our case to the Father

III. Four confessions taught in the New Testament
   A. Confession of sin under the old covenant
   B. Confession of the sinner today
   C. Confession of sin by the believer
   D. Confession of faith in the Word, in Christ and in God the Father

IV. What believers are to confess
   A. God's plan of redemption for us
   B. What the Holy Spirit is doing in us
   C. What we are to God in Christ
   D. What Jesus is doing for us now
   E. What God can do through us

Study Questions

(1) How do we release faith? _____

_____

_____

_____

(2) Why is it so important to speak words based on God's Word? ____

_____

_____

_____

_____

(3) According to Hebrews 3:1, what is Jesus to us? _____

_____

_____

_____

_____

(4) What four confessions are taught in the New Testament? _____

_____

_____

_____

_____

(5) As believers, what five confessions should we make? _____

_____

_____

_____

_____

Study Notes

"...As it is written, I believed, and therefore have I spoken;
we also believe, and therefore speak."
2 Corinthians 4:13

"And seeing a fig tree...he found nothing but leaves.... And Jesus answered and said unto it, No man eat fruit of thee hereafter for ever.... And in the morning, as they passed by, they saw the fig tree dried up from the roots."

Mark 11:13-14, 20

Jesus has the God kind of faith.
He speaks the end result and sees it come to pass.
So can you.

CD FOUR
First Principles of faith I

Having the God Kind of Faith Means Acting as God Would—God Always Speaks the Desired End Result, Not the Circumstances

"*H*ave [the God kind of faith].
For verily I say unto you, That whosoever
shall say unto this mountain...he shall have
whatsoever he saith."

(Mark 11:22-23)

Release the Force of Faith

FOCUS: "Whosoever shall say unto this mountain, Be thou removed, and be thou cast into the sea; and shall not doubt in his heart..." (Mark 11:23).

In Mark 11, Jesus demonstrated how to use faith. He approached the fig tree and said, "No man eat fruit of thee hereafter for ever" (verse 14). The words He spoke cursed the tree. He did not say, "Fig tree, I curse you." He did not say anything to the tree except *the desired end result*. From that moment on, Jesus did not mention the tree again. He went about His business and His faith kept on working.

The next day, as Jesus and His disciples passed by the tree, they saw it dried up from the roots. Peter brought it to the attention of Jesus, but He still did not make a direct comment concerning the tree. In fact, He never spoke about it again. He only told them how it was accomplished.

Jesus gave them the *law of faith* as outlined in Mark 11:22-25: "And Jesus answering saith unto them, Have faith in God [Or, Have the faith of God]. For verily I say unto you, That whosoever shall say unto this mountain, Be thou removed, and be thou cast into the sea; and shall not doubt in his heart, but shall believe that those things which he saith shall come to pass; he shall have whatsoever he saith. Therefore I say unto you, What things soever ye desire, when ye pray, believe that ye receive them, and ye shall have them. And when ye stand praying, forgive, if ye have aught against any: that your Father also which is in heaven may forgive you your tresspasses." This is a good example of the fact that spiritual power is actually governed and controlled by spiritual law.

Release the force of faith by speaking the desired end result.

The Bible is a copy of the words God used to release His faith into the earth. When God said, "Let there be light" and "Let there be..." all the other things He spoke into existence, they became reality. He did it all with the force of faith.

It's a powerful force. Jesus said that a grain of faith the size of a mustard seed can move a mountain (Luke 17:6). That's why He said, "Have the faith of God." Take the Words of God, feed your heart with them, and let them come out of your mouth. The force of faith will flood out of your lips too.

Jesus said in the Gospel of Mark, *"Whosoever* shall say...." Apply your faith to the situation. It will work for you like it worked for Jesus. *Release the force of faith by speaking the desired end result.*

When Peter ministered to the lame man, he spoke only the desired end result: "In the name of Jesus Christ of Nazareth rise up and walk" (Acts 3:6). What happened? Immediately his feet and ankle bones received strength, and he leaped up and entered the temple praising God. Peter released the force of faith on his behalf.

But there is more involved here than just speaking words. Mark 11:23 continues with "...and shall not doubt in his heart." Faith is of the heart, not the mind. Words without the force of faith are void of power. And if you are trying to base your faith on what looks reasonable according to the world's standards, you will become double-minded.

Make a decision to judge all things according to the Word. Then you will get to the place where what God says to you in His Word is more reasonable than natural thinking.

Faith Will Not Work in an Unforgiving Heart

FOCUS: "And when ye stand praying, forgive, if ye have aught against any..." (Mark 11:25).

When you are walking in unforgiveness, you are not in agreement with God. You are not in agreement with His Word. He gave Jesus for you so that you could be free from your debt of sin. If you are holding something against someone, release it and let it go. Free them from their debt to you. Unforgiveness is sin. When you confess it to the Father, He will forgive you and cleanse you from all unrighteousness (1 John 1:8).

Faith works by love (Galatians 5:6). The love of God is the greatest motivation behind the force of faith. In the Bible, we see that love is what motivated God to use His faith to create the universe and man. Love is the power charge that undergirds the force of faith. The force of love is the reason that faith works. So learn to walk in love. ☙

Faith is of the heart, not the head. Romans 10:10 says it is with the heart that man believes. So it's important to feed your heart (your spirit)

Now Begin Enjoying It

Second Corinthians 4:16 says, "The inward man is renewed day by day." Just as the body needs physical food and the mind needs intellectual food, the spirit needs spiritual food. God's Word is the spiritual food that produces the power of faith (Romans 10:17), so feed on the Word. The more Word you "eat," the stronger your inner man will become. Then faith will constantly be at work within you to meet every need.

CD 4 Outlined

I. Jesus demonstrated the law of faith
   A. He spoke to the fig tree (Mark 11:12-14)
   B. He spoke the desired end result
   C. He never mentioned the tree again, but His faith
      continued to work

II. Jesus outlined the law of faith in Mark 11:22-26
   A. "Whosoever shall say..."
      1. Speak faith to your situation
      2. Speak the desired end result
   B. "And shall not doubt in his heart, but shall believe"
      1. Words without the force of faith are void of power
      2. Base faith on the Word, not human ideas

III. Faith will not work in an unforgiving heart
   A. God gave Jesus to set us free from our debt of
      sin—He has forgiven us
   B. Confess (to God) the sin of unforgiveness
   C. When you stand praying, forgive (Mark 11:25-26)

IV. Faith works by love (Galatians 5:6)
   A. The love of God is the greatest motivation behind the
      force of faith
   B. The force of love is the reason that faith works

V. Faith is of the heart, not the mind
   A. With the heart man believes (Romans 10:10)
   B. The inward man is renewed day by day (2 Corinthians 4:16)
      1. The Word produces faith in the heart (Romans 10:17)

Study Questions

(1) What did Jesus do to demonstrate how to use faith? _____

_____

_____

_____

(2) When you apply faith-filled words to a situation, what should

you speak? _____

_____

_____

_____

(3) How can you keep from being double-minded? _____

_____

_____

_____

_____

_____

(4) Why is it so important to be forgiving? _____

_____

_____

_____

_____

_____

Study Notes

"So then faith cometh by hearing, and hearing by the word of God."
Romans 10:17

"Therefore be imitators of God [copy Him and follow His example] as well-beloved children [imitate their father]."

Ephesians 5:1, *The Amplified Bible*

To imitate your Father God...
begin living by faith.

CD FIVE
First Principles of Faith II

Every Born-Again Believer Has the God Kind of Faith— It's Up to Us to Make Faith Our Lifestyle

"*I*beseech you therefore, brethren...*to every man that is among you....* God hath dealt to every man the measure of faith."

Romans 12:1-3

Follow Jesus' Example

FOCUS: "As my Father hath taught me, I speak
these things...for I do always those things that please him"
(John 8:28-29).

We are told in Ephesians 5:1 to be followers of God as dear children. The word *follower* means "imitator." We are to imitate God as children imitate their earthly parents.

We see a perfect example of this in the life of Jesus. Jesus said that He does the same as His Father does and speaks only the things that the Father has taught Him (John 5:19, 8:28). He is the express image of God. We know about God's character by looking at Jesus.

Jesus operated totally by faith. He spoke words full of power. In every situation, He spoke the desired end result. He spoke the words of God (John 3:34). The manifestation of what He spoke came to pass because He operated exactly like God.

God spoke the inner image on the inside of Himself and there was light...there was dry land...there were beasts of the field...there was man. God brought what existed in the spiritual world into the realm of the five physical senses, and He did it by faith. That's the God kind of faith. Did you know that it's available to you...if you're a believer?

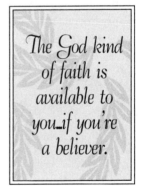

The God kind of faith is available to you...if you're a believer.

Second Thessalonians 3:2 says, "All men have not faith."

But in writing to the church at Rome, Paul said, "I beseech you therefore, *brethren*...through the grace given unto me, to every man that is *among you,* not to think of himself more highly than he ought to think; but to think soberly, according as God hath dealt *to every man* the measure of faith" (Romans 12:1-3). Paul was talking to Christians in this passage of Scripture. He was saying that every born-again believer has been given the faith of God. He received it at the very moment he accepted Jesus as Lord. It is his to use. ༄

It's important to base your faith on what the Word says about any situation. Living by faith is a way of life for the believer. So begin to feed your inner man with the Word of God until he becomes strong.

Now Begin Enjoying It

Make confessions based on the Word. Let the Word be your motivation. As you do, the Spirit of God will make that Word a living reality in you. The result will be God's power made available to bring forth fruit in your life.

CD 5 Outlined

I. Be a follower of God (Ephesians 5:1)
   A. *Follower* means "imitator"
   B. Jesus was the express image of God
   C. His ministry expressed God's character
      1. God's character is faith
      2. God the Father and Jesus spoke things into existence with faith-filled words
      3. Jesus spoke the words of God (John 3:34)

II. Who has the God kind of faith?
   A. The born-again believer
      1. Every born-again believer has been dealt the measure of faith (Romans 12:1-3)
      2. It is the gift of God
      3. He can use it as his own

III. How to release faith
   A. The primary way: With the words of the mouth
   B. God's faith-filled words create

Study Questions

(1) What does it mean to be a follower of God? _____

_____

_____

_____

(2) Who has the God kind of faith? _____

_____

_____

_____

_____

(3) What is the primary way to release faith? _____

_____

_____

_____

_____

(4) Why should we be selective of the words we speak? _____

_____

_____

_____

_____

(5) How are we able to control what we say? _____

_____

_____

_____

Study Notes

"Be ye therefore followers of God, as dear children;
and walk in love, as Christ also hath loved us...."

Ephesians 5:1-2

6

"Death and life are in the power of the tongue...."

Proverbs 18:21

Words are containers.
They can carry life or death.
It's up to us to fill them with life.

CD SIX
First Principles of Faith III

"My son, attend to my words.... For they are life unto those that find them.... Put away from thee a froward mouth, and perverse lips put far from thee."
Proverbs 4:20-24

Words Are Containers

FOCUS: "Death and life are in the power of the tongue: and they that love it shall eat the fruit thereof" (Proverbs 18:21).

Whether you know it or not, all the words you speak are carrying *something*. Words can carry fear and hate (being instruments of destruction), or they can carry love and faith—bringing life to all those who hear.

Words are the most powerful weapons on earth. Not only do they affect others, but they control the course of our own lives. Use words that build up and edify.

Negative confessions will only bring defeat. So make the decision to speak faith, based on the Word.

Jesus gave the principle of faith in Mark 11:22-26. In verse 23 He said: "That whosoever shall say unto this mountain, Be thou removed, and be thou cast into the sea; and shall not doubt in his heart, but shall believe that those things which he *saith* shall come to pass; he shall have whatsoever he *saith*." Notice that He said, "*...those things* which he *saith*." Jesus was talking about all the things we say.

Every word that comes out of your mouth has the power to directly affect your life for good or for bad. James 3:10-11 says, "Out of the same mouth proceedeth blessing and cursing. My brethren, these things ought not so to be. Doth a fountain send forth at the same place sweet water and bitter?" Determine to bring your entire vocabulary in line with the Word of God and under the leadership of the Holy Spirit. To do this: *Feed your spirit with the Word of God.*

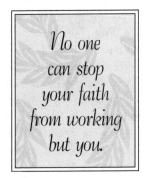

No one can stop your faith from working but you.

As you feed on the Word and let it nourish your inner man, the image on the inside of you will begin to change. Your confession will come in line with the will of God. The strength of God will come up from deep within and it will come out of your mouth. You will speak words of life. You will speak from your spirit where the forces of life reside.

Proverbs 4:20-23 says: "My son, attend to my words; incline thine ear unto my sayings. Let them not depart from thine eyes; keep them in the midst of thine heart. For they are life unto those that find them, and health to all their flesh. Keep thy heart with all diligence; for out of it are the issues of life."

Give your full attention to the Word of God. It is the most important thing. It is life to you! That's why Proverbs 15:4 says, "A wholesome tongue is a tree of life."

The World of the Spirit Is a Higher Level of Existence

FOCUS: "For as the heavens are higher than the earth, so are my ways higher than your ways, and my thoughts than your thoughts" (Isaiah 55:9).

The natural world makes its decisions based on the five physical senses—sight, hearing, touch, taste and smell. Faith, however, is based on what the Word of God says. Faith sees what the Word of God says—the eye of faith sees the victory.

From faith comes the seen world. The physical is a result of the spiritual. Temporal things are subject to change—God's Word is the same (Hebrews 13:8). You can depend on it!

Faith in the established Word works, both in prayer, and by saying only—without praying. As you speak God's Word in faith, His power is available to bring that Word to pass.

As you operate the law of faith, you are in the position to receive from God. Peter used his faith *on purpose* on behalf of the beggar at the gate Beautiful. He said: "Silver and gold have I none; but such as I have give I thee: In the name of Jesus Christ of Nazareth rise up and walk" (Acts 3:6). Peter was using his faith in the Name of Jesus on behalf of someone else. He did not pray—he made a faith command in the Name of Jesus and the Word was performed. Jesus' Name, through faith, made the man whole. In verse 12, Peter explains it was not his calling and his office as an apostle that made this possible. It was his faith as a believer that put the Word to work.

Faith does not work apart from God. It is impossible to please Him without faith. We use the power He has given us to activate the Word in our lives as well as in the lives of others. That is part of the commandment to the Church in 1 John 3:23. God will honor our faith because He honors the Name of Jesus. When we speak to sickness and disease, it is faith in the Name that will put a stop to their effects. His Name is above every name.

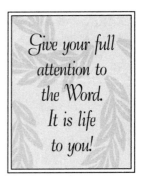

Give your full attention to the Word. It is life to you!

Faith will always work for you. *No one can stop your faith from working but you.* If you allow yourself to listen to outside influences, the opportunity will present itself to waver and turn your faith off. But as you resist those things that are contrary to the Word you are activating, the Word will be the result.

Most of the time your faith will also work for someone else. But there comes a time when they must stand on their own faith and believe God for themselves. ✑

When applying your faith, go to the Word. You can have confidence that you are in total harmony with God's will in every situation. He cannot honor what you speak or believe for outside of the Word.

Now Begin Enjoying It

The Word of God is the handbook of life. It has the answer for every need of mankind. So find out what the Word says about your situation. Let that be what you see by the eye of faith, and say all the time...and get ready to receive.

CD 6 Outlined

I. Words are containers
   A. They carry life or death (Proverbs 18:21)
   B. Words are the most powerful weapons
   C. Words set the course of our lives

II. Faith is based on eternal things
   A. Eternal things in the unseen realm
   B. The Word is eternal
   C. From faith comes the seen world

III. Faith works outside of prayer—in every realm of life
   A. Peter and the beggar (Acts 3:6)
   B. Jesus raised the widow's son (Luke 7:14)

IV. Faith works in prayer
   A. Peter raised Tabitha (Acts 9:40)
   B. Jesus raised Lazarus (John 11:41-43)

V. Faith does not work apart from God

VI. Faith will always work
   A. No one can stop your faith but you
   B. Your faith must be based on God's will
      1. His will is His Word

Study Questions

(1) What does faith have to be based on to work? _____

_____

_____

_____

(2) Give an example of faith working by speaking only. _____

_____

_____

_____

_____

(3) Give an example of faith working in prayer. _____

_____

_____

_____

_____

_____

(4) Why does faith in the Name of Jesus work? _____

_____

_____

_____

(5) Who can stop your faith and how? _____

_____

_____

_____

_____

Study Notes

"Keep thy heart with all diligence; for out of it are the issues of life."
Proverbs 4:23

"Through faith we understand that the worlds were framed by the word of God."

Hebrews 11:3

God released His faith with His words...
and the unseen became the seen.

CD SEVEN
Developing the Spirit of Faith

"Now faith is the substance
of things hoped for, the evidence
of things not seen. For by it the
elders obtained a good report. Through
faith we understand
that the worlds were framed by
the word of God, so that things which are
seen were not made
of things which do appear."
Hebrews 11:1-3

*I*n this study, learn to develop the
force of faith in your own life.

Faith Is the Force God Used to Create Everything You Can See

FOCUS: "Faith is the substance of things hoped for.... Through faith we understand that the worlds were framed by the word of God" (Hebrews 11:1-3).

"And the earth was without form, and void; and darkness was upon the face of the deep. And the Spirit of God moved upon the face of the waters. And God said, Let there be light: and there was light" (Genesis 1:2-3).

In Genesis 1, the Spirit of God was moving upon the face of the waters. But it was not until God spoke, and released the substance of His faith, that we see creation in manifestation. As God spoke, the Holy Spirit took the substance of faith that resided in God's words and performed what He said. God's words were the instruments that released the faith that framed the worlds. God knew, without doubt, that the desired end result would be manifested. He had faith in His faith.

Since faith is the parent force of all that exists, the natural world will respond to faith. Everything that we can contact with the five physical senses is subject to the force of faith. The only problem is learning to release it.

God released faith into the earth. He gave faith to Adam and expected him to use it. As God's underruler, Adam was to use this faith to keep his surroundings and circumstances in line with God. But he failed to do that.

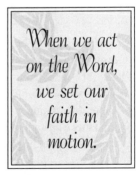

When we act on the Word, we set our faith in motion.

Adam committed high treason and put his faith into the hand of a foreign god who perverted it and turned it into a negative force—fear. When Adam sinned, fear became the dominant force in his life.

God was left on the outside of the earth looking in. He had to find a legal entry back into the affairs of man.

At that time, no one on earth had, by nature, the force of faith operating in them. They could come up with a level of confidence and faith that was very strong, but it was a highly developed human faith. The Bible says that Abraham's faith was of that kind. That was the best faith he could come up with, and God accepted it and accounted it unto him for righteousness. A blood covenant was cut—a covenant that not only gave God His avenue back into the earth, but established promises between God and His people that we, as believers, partake of today.

Jesus came, defeated Satan, and took the authority from him that was originally Adam's. He reinstated man in a position of fellowship with God. Those who accepted Jesus through faith became born again, and they were made the righteousness of God. The God kind of faith took up residence in their hearts. Hebrews 12:2 says Jesus is "the author and finisher [or Developer] of our faith." He reintroduced it into the earth.

How Can We Develop the Force of Faith?

FOCUS: Jesus [the Word] is "the author and finisher [or Developer] of our faith" (Hebrews 12:2).

Every force, or fruit, of the reborn human spirit is developed and brought to perfection by putting the Word of God first place.

The first step to putting the Word first place is *meditation in the Word of God.* Meditation is more than just studying or reading the Bible. Meditation is fixing your mind on the Word. Verse by verse, let the Holy Spirit paint a picture on the inside of you until you have a clear understanding of what is being said. He will reveal the truth.

Joshua, upon replacing Moses, was instructed of God to meditate the Word day and night so he could see how to do the job set before him—lead the Israelites. God's wisdom in the Word would enable him to deal wisely in every situation. "This book of the law shall not depart out of thy mouth; but thou shalt meditate therein day and night, that thou mayest observe to do according to all that is written therein: for then thou shalt make thy way prosperous, and then thou shalt have good success" (Joshua 1:8).

The second step to putting the Word first place is to *act on the Word*. James said to be a *doer* of the Word and not a hearer only (James 1:22). When we act on the Word, we set our faith in motion. The more we act on the Word, the more we develop our faith. We saw earlier that Jesus is the Developer of our faith. As we act on the Word, we put our faith in His hands, and He's able to do something with it. But when we quit acting, there's nothing He can do. If we stop activating our faith, the Word will not work.

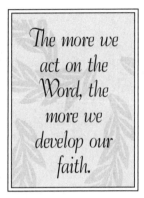

The more we act on the Word, the more we develop our faith.

Act on the Word as quickly as you would the word of your doctor, best friend or lawyer. By acting on the Word you are saying, "God, I know You are not a liar. I can put my complete trust in You."

Now Begin Enjoying It

Do not look in the Scriptures for the things you must not do; look for the things you can do. You can do all things through Christ which strengthens you (Philippians 4:13). Christ is at work in you, strengthening you, enabling you to handle the circumstances of life with confidence in the Word.

CD 7 Outlined

I. The spoken Word produced for God (Genesis 1:1-3)
   A. Faith was the substance in God's words (Hebrews 11:1-3
   B. Faith-filled words put the Holy Spirit into action
   C. Faith is the parent force of all that exists

II. God gave Adam faith to use

III. Adam committed high treason and changed gods
   A. Adam's faith was replaced by fear when he fell
   B. God was left on the outside of the earth

IV. God approached Abram—a way back into man's affairs
   A. Abraham believed God and accepted the
      covenant in faith
   B. Abraham had highly developed human faith
   C. It was accounted to him for righteousness

V. Jesus reinstated man in a position of fellowship
   with God.
   A. Those who accept Jesus are born again and
      made righteous
   B. The God kind of faith takes up residence in
      their hearts
   C. Jesus is the author and finisher, or developer, of
      our faith (Hebrews 12:2)

VI. How to develop the force of faith
   A. Put the Word first place
      1. Meditation—fix your mind on the Word (Joshua 1:8)
      2. Act on what the Word says

Study Questions

(1) Why is faith the parent force of all that exists? _____

_____

_____

_____

(2) What is the difference between a born-again believer's faith and the faith of Abraham? _____

_____

_____

_____

(3) Where is the force of faith developed? _____

_____

_____

_____

(4) What can we do to develop the force of faith? _____

_____

_____

_____

(5) What are the two ways of putting the Word first place? _____

_____

_____

_____

Study Notes

"I can do all things through Christ which strengtheneth me."
Philippians 4:13

8

"So then faith cometh by
hearing, and hearing by the
word of God."

Romans 10:17

Faith only comes one way...
by hearing the Word of God.

CD EIGHT
Faith Cometh by Hearing

"But the righteousness which is of faith speaketh on this wise...The word is nigh thee, even in thy mouth, and in thy heart: that is, the word of faith, which we preach; that if thou shalt confess with thy mouth the Lord Jesus, and shalt believe in thine heart that God hath raised him from the dead, thou shalt be saved. For with the heart man believeth unto righteousness; and with the mouth confession is made unto salvation. For the scripture saith, Whosoever believeth on him shall not be ashamed.... So then faith cometh by hearing, and hearing by the word of God."

(Romans 10:6-11, 17)

Faith Is Active and It Can Be Developed...but It Only Comes One Way

FOCUS: "So then faith cometh by hearing, and hearing by the word of God" (Romans 10:17).

When the Word is heard, the Spirit of God illuminates that Word, and your faith begins to grow and develop. This faith of God that resides on the inside of you is as close as the breath in your mouth. If you release it, it will come out. Romans 10:6-8 says, "But the righteousness which is of faith speaketh...what saith it? The word is nigh thee, even in thy mouth, and in thy heart: that is, the word of faith, which we preach."

To be heard, faith must be released by the mouth. God released faith in His words—not just some of them—but every word. That is why faith comes when we hear the Word of God preached. It is filled with the faith of God.

Sinners get saved the same way—by hearing the word of faith—by believing and confessing Jesus is Lord with their mouths.

Faith is based on what the Word says, not on physical manifestations. Remember, we're walking by faith, not by sight (2 Corinthians 5:7). To say, "Lord, touch me with Your nail-scarred hand" is reaching into an area of the natural to contact the spiritual. It will not work.

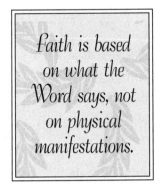

Faith is based on what the Word says, not on physical manifestations.

As a spirit being, you contact God in the spiritual realm. "God is a Spirit: and they that worship him must worship him in spirit and in truth" (John 4:23). Colossians 3:1-2 says, "If ye then be risen with Christ, seek those things which are above, where Christ sitteth on the right hand of God. Set your affection on things above, not on things on the earth."

In Romans 10:6-8, we see an example of faith based on the Word instead of physical manifestation: "But the righteousness which is of faith speaketh on this wise, Say not in thine heart, Who shall ascend into heaven? (that is, to bring Christ down from above:) Or, Who shall descend into the deep? (that is, to bring up Christ again from the dead). But what saith it? The word is nigh thee, even in thy mouth, and in thy heart: that is, the word of faith, which we preach."

Jesus does not need to come down from heaven to meet our needs. He does not need to die and be resurrected again. His work was complete.

He gave us all power and authority and His Name to use. We have been invested with God's ability. We can do the same works that Jesus did in His earthly ministry, but we must use the same principle He used. He applied faith to what the Father God said. In the same way, our faith-filled words, based on the Word, will produce results.

The Word shows us that faith comes to "whosoever." It comes to the human heart that hears and receives the Word. It is not given to a select few because of their calling. You see, God is not a respecter of persons. He honors His Word. Mark 11:23 states, "That *whosoever* shall say...," and Romans 10:13 says, "For *whosoever* shall call upon the name of the Lord shall be saved." It is available to all.

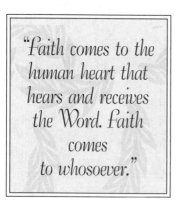

"*Faith comes to the human heart that hears and receives the Word. Faith comes to whosoever.*"

But Second Timothy 2:20-21 says there are different kinds of vessels: "But in a great house there are not only vessels of gold and of silver, but also of wood and of earth; and some to honour, and some to dishonour. If a man therefore purge himself from these, he shall be a vessel unto honour, sanctified, and meet for the master's use, and prepared unto every good work."

The Word of God says that we can be vessels of honor in this great house and be separated, sanctified and able to be used by the Master. Every Christian endeavor we launch should succeed and bear fruit. But we have to purge ourselves to be usable.

The purging is not done by God, but by the believer through the washing of water—by the Word. When the Word is applied, it purifies and makes whole. ✎

We cannot depend on our own human ability. This is done by the power of God—but we still have to apply the Word. We still have to use our faith.

Now Begin Enjoying It

Romans 1:17 says, "The just shall live by faith." Make the decision to put your dependence and your faith in the ability of the Word of God, the Name of Jesus, the Holy Spirit and the corporate structure of heaven that is behind the Word.

The faith that is in the Word of God will come, and you will walk in all boldness and confidence. Make the decision that you are what the Word says you are and you can do what the Word says you can do. Remember, faith in the Word will always put you over.

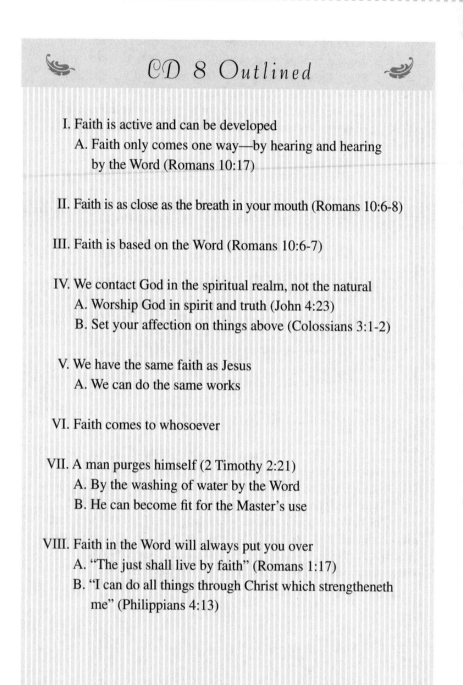

ℭ𝒟 8 Outlined

I. Faith is active and can be developed
   A. Faith only comes one way—by hearing and hearing
     by the Word (Romans 10:17)

II. Faith is as close as the breath in your mouth (Romans 10:6-8)

III. Faith is based on the Word (Romans 10:6-7)

IV. We contact God in the spiritual realm, not the natural
   A. Worship God in spirit and truth (John 4:23)
   B. Set your affection on things above (Colossians 3:1-2)

V. We have the same faith as Jesus
   A. We can do the same works

VI. Faith comes to whosoever

VII. A man purges himself (2 Timothy 2:21)
   A. By the washing of water by the Word
   B. He can become fit for the Master's use

VIII. Faith in the Word will always put you over
   A. "The just shall live by faith" (Romans 1:17)
   B. "I can do all things through Christ which strengtheneth
     me" (Philippians 4:13)

Study Questions

(1) How does faith come? _____

_____

_____

_____

(2) What does "righteousness which is of faith" say? _____

_____

_____

_____

(3) Why is is unnecessary for Jesus to come down from heaven or to be resurrected again? _____

_____

_____

_____

_____

(4) Who does faith come to? _____

_____

_____

_____

(5) What must be done in order for a man to be a vessel unto honor?

_____

_____

_____

Study Notes

"For therein is the righteousness of God revealed from faith to faith; as it is written, The just shall live by faith."

Romans 1:17

"Blessed are they that
have not seen, and yet
have believed."

John 20:29

The greatest faith accepts the Word alone...
without any evidence.

CD NINE
The Greatest Faith

The Highest Form of Faith Is to Believe Entirely on the Word of God and Its Authority Alone, Without Any Physical Evidence to Support

"The centurion answered and said, Lord, I am not worthy that thou shouldest come under my roof: but *speak the word only,* and my servant shall be healed."

Matthew 8:8

Great Faith Rests Confidently in the Authority and Power of What God Has Said

FOCUS: "The centurion answered...speak the word only, and my servant shall be healed.... When Jesus heard it, he marvelled, and said to them that followed, Verily I say unto you, I have not found so great faith, no, not in Israel" (Matthew 8:8-10).

In Matthew 8, there is the story of a centurion whose servant was afflicted with palsy. When he approached Jesus and implored Him for the health of his servant, Jesus told the centurion He would come and heal him. "The centurion answered and said, Lord, I am not worthy that thou shouldest come under my roof: but speak *the word only,* and my servant shall be healed" (Matthew 8:8). He continued by explaining that he was a man under authority and that he had others under his authority. He said that when he spoke, those under his authority did what he said.

Jesus was amazed and said that this man had "great faith." If anyone knows about faith, it is Jesus—the author of our faith. He recognized that the man was using his faith just as Jesus was accustomed to do. In verse 13, Jesus spoke, and the servant was healed in the selfsame hour. It was done exactly the way the centurion believed.

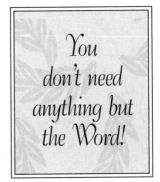

You don't need anything but the Word!

This is an example of the highest form of faith. The centurion recognized the authority in the words of Jesus, and he based his belief solely on His words. He didn't require any physical evidence to support the truth. He simply believed that what Jesus spoke would come to pass.

When Jesus spoke, He had confidence that His words would not return void, but they would come to pass. He is the author of this kind of faith.

We see Him on the Mount of Temptation when Satan tried to get Him to prove that He was the Son of God. He didn't rely on any physical evidence to tell Him that God's Word was true. He answered Satan by saying, "It is written, Man shall not live by bread alone, but by every word that proceedeth out of the mouth of God" (Matthew 4:4).

In Luke 10, Jesus told Martha that Mary, in choosing to hear the Word rather than to help serve the guests, had chosen the "good part, which shall not be taken away from her" (verse 42). He said that only one thing was necessary—the Word of God. He was saying to her, "You don't need anything but the Word!"

The Word of God is spirit and life, and it will bring life to any situation (John 6:63).

Believing the Word is faith in action. The five physical senses are not the evidence of the Word at work. Faith is perceiving as real fact that which has not been revealed to the senses. It's the "title deed" to what you're believing for (Hebrews 11:1, *The Amplified Bible*). Receiving the Word as true, believing it, acting on it, and confessing it is reaching into the world of the spirit and drawing it into the reality of the here and now. God's Word will not return void (Isaiah 55:11).

> *faith is the "title deed" to what you're believing for.*

The lowest form of faith is depending on the physical sense realm to be the evidence of God's Word at work. This is believing because you see.

In John 20:25, Thomas said that unless he could see the nail prints in Jesus' hands and touch His wounds, *he would not believe* that Jesus had risen from the dead. As an act of his will, Thomas chose to believe sense knowledge.

When Jesus appeared to the disciples again, He gave Thomas the opportunity to see and touch Him. Then Jesus said, "Be not faithless, but believing" (John 20:27). He went on to say, "Thomas, because thou hast seen me, thou hast believed: blessed are they that have not seen, and yet have believed" (verse 29). The person who believes God *as an act of his faith,* on purpose, is the one who is blessed. Faith doesn't come by divine visions or appearances. Faith comes by hearing and hearing by the Word of God (Romans 10:17). So commit to take the Word of God as your only evidence. ◦◦◦

The Christian who has separated what he perceives through his senses from what the Word says has put himself in a position for his faith to grow and mature.

Now Begin Enjoying It

Faith reaches its highest when you have not seen but you believe on purpose. So *take hold of the Word,* even though you can see no other evidence causing you to believe. When you make the decision to believe God's Word without any sense evidence, there is no limit to the heights your faith can reach.

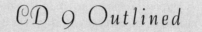

CD 9 Outlined

I. There are two kinds of knowledge
   A. Sense realm knowledge: What is perceived through the five physical senses
   B. Revelation knowledge: What is perceived spiritually from the Word of God

II. The highest form of faith
   A. Faith in God's Word alone, with no physical evidence
   B. Recognition of the authority of God's Word
   C. Belief based on that authority

III. The Word of God is spirit and life (John 6:63)
   A. Man does not live by bread alone but by the Word of God (Matthew 4:4)
   B. Faith is receiving as fact the Word of God even when it has not been revealed to the senses

IV. The lowest form of faith
   A. An attitude of "seeing is believing"
   B. Physical evidence is required in order to believe

V. Faith can be developed and matured
   A. Make the Word final authority
   B. Accept the Word as the only evidence

Study Questions

(1) Explain the difference between sense knowledge and revelation knowledge. _____

_____

_____

_____

(2) What is the highest form of faith? _____

_____

_____

_____

(3) Why did Jesus marvel at the centurion's faith? _____

_____

_____

_____

_____

(4) What is the lowest form of faith? _____

_____

_____

_____

(5) How can you place yourself in the position for your faith to develop and mature? _____

_____

_____

_____

Study Notes

"So shall my word be that goeth forth out of my mouth:
it shall not return unto me void, but it shall accomplish that which
I please, and it shall prosper in the thing whereto I sent it."
Isaiah 55:11

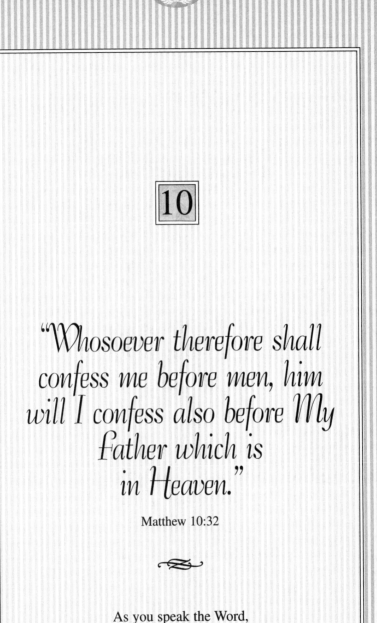

10

"Whosoever therefore shall
confess me before men, him
will I confess also before My
Father which is
in Heaven."

Matthew 10:32

As you speak the Word,
Jesus confesses it before the Father.

CD TEN
Five Basic Confessions

Spoken out of Your Mouth, the Word of God Will Bring Life to Every Area of Your Existence

"**S**eeing then that we have a great high priest,
that is passed into the
heavens, Jesus the Son of God, *let us
hold fast our profession.*"

Hebrews 4:14

The Word of God Is Alive and Full of Power

FOCUS: "For the word of God is quick [alive], and powerful, and sharper than any twoedged sword, piercing even to the dividing asunder of soul and spirit, and of the joints and marrow, and is a discerner of the thoughts and intents of the heart" (Hebrews 4:12). The Word covers the entire spectrum of human existence.

God sent His Word into the earth to build our faith and confidence in Him. As we gain knowledge of the Word, our confession of that Word will release our faith and put it to work.

God has given us His Word, written on paper, so that we can build it into our spirits, our joints, and the very marrow of our bones can be filled with the living Word of God—to the point where that Word will come rolling across our lips in the form of a confession. That confession will build a solid front before us called the shield of faith, which we can use to quench every fiery dart that the enemy throws at us.

Jesus said we are to hold fast the profession of our faith without wavering (Hebrews 4:14, 10:23). We do not confess Jesus out one side of our mouth and then confess weakness, sickness, failure or lack out the other side. We are to hold fast our confession of the Word of God.

Do not be afraid to confess the revelation you have received from God's Word. Being afraid to confess the Word of God before you can see the manifestation you're believing for is to doubt the integrity of God and His Word.

We are to hold fast to our confession.

Jesus said, "What I tell you in darkness, that speak ye in light: and what ye hear in the ear, that preach ye upon the housetops.... Whosoever therefore shall confess me before men, him will I confess also before my Father which is in heaven" (Matthew 10:27, 32). As you speak the Word, Jesus confesses it before the Father because He is the High Priest of our confession (Hebrews 3:1).

Confessing the Word puts God's power to work in your behalf. The shield of faith quenches all the fiery darts of the wicked.

Now Begin Enjoying It

As you bring your vocabulary in line with the Word, it will begin ordering your life. You'll find that your actions will begin to be in obedience to God. Your life will begin to be ordered of God.

So order the words of your mouth. Make a decision to commit your lips totally to speaking only the truth of God's Word.

The following are five basic confessions to hold fast:

*1. Jesus is Lord over (your need)*_____.
Confess the absolute lordship of Jesus Christ. Every believer gave Jesus the right to be his Lord when he became born again. Satan no longer has any rights to his life. But when Jesus became Lord, He didn't just become Lord over the Church. He became Lord over *all*. Sickness, disease, poverty, marital problems, strife and any other work of Satan has to bow its knee to the lordship of Jesus (see Philippians 2:9-11). Jesus exercises His lordship over the kingdom of Satan through you and me as we use His Name and exercise our authority in our Lord Jesus Christ: "I make Jesus Lord over this situation." You bring Jesus on the scene instantly when you confess His lordship.

2. I do not have a care. First Peter 5:6-7 says to humble yourself by casting all your care upon God. God will not humble you; you humble yourself. When all care, worry and concern are cast on God, then a man has come under the authority of the Word and made it first place in his life.

3. The Lord is my Shepherd, I do not want. All my needs are met. Salvation, healing, financial ability and anything else a person could need already belong to the believer through Jesus Christ. We are seated at the table of abundance in the presence of our enemies now, in this lifetime (Psalm 23).

4. I am free. The child of God is free from the power of Satan. All that Adam turned over to him in the Garden of Eden has been bought back by Jesus. Satan has no more dominion over you. Sickness, lack, grief, habits, sin, etc., are under the curse of the law. You are free from all those things because they were laid on Jesus (see Isaiah 53:3-5). You have been redeemed from the curse of the law (Galatians 3:13-14). Whom the Son sets free is free indeed (John 8:36).

5. Jesus is made unto me wisdom, righteousness, sanctification and redemption (1 Corinthians 1:30).
As joint heirs with Jesus, everything He has belongs to us. The promises were made *to* us and *for* us. They are rightfully ours because we have right-standing with God. The Word is our bill of rights.

CD 10 Outlined

I. The Word of God is alive and full of power
   A. Hebrews 4:12
   B. When you speak it out of your mouth, it brings life
      to every area of your existence

II. Confession of the Word releases faith and puts it to work

III. Jesus said to hold fast your profession of faith without wavering
   A. Don't speak the Word out one side of your mouth
      and negative things out the other side
   B. Hold fast the confession of the Word of God

IV. Don't be afraid to confess revelation from God's Word
   A. Being afraid to confess the Word before you see the
      manifestation is doubting the integrity of God and
      His Word
   B. The Word you confess, Jesus confesses before the
      Father (Matthew 10:27, 32)
   C. Jesus is High Priest of our confession (Hebrews 3:1)

V. Speak God's Word
   A. Commit to the truth
   B. Confessing the Word puts God's power to work in
      your behalf

VI. Five basic confessions to hold fast
   A. Jesus is Lord over *all* (Philippians 2:9-11)
   B. I do not have a care (1 Peter 5:6-7)
   C. The Lord is my Shepherd, I do not want (Psalm 23)
   D. I am free (John 8:36)
   E. Jesus is made unto me wisdom, righteousness,
      sanctification and redemption (1 Corinthians 1:30)

Study Questions

(1) How does the Word affect our faith? _____

_____

_____

_____

(2) Why is it necessary to confess what God has revealed to you? _____

_____

_____

_____

(3) What is the result of being afraid to confess God's Word?_____

_____

_____

_____

_____

(4) Give the five basic confessions. _____

_____

_____

_____

_____

_____

(5) What does making Jesus Lord really mean?_____

_____

_____

_____

_____

Study Notes

"Let us hold fast the profession of our faith without wavering;
(for he is faithful that promised)."
Hebrews 10:23

11

"Trust in the Lord
with all thine heart; and lean
not unto thine
own understanding."

Proverbs 3:5

Establish your trust—your heart—on God and His
Word...not your own human understanding.

CD ELEVEN
The Established Heart

A Believer Can Have the Things of God and the Power of God Working in His Life When His Heart Is Established in the Word and He Is Trusting in the Lord

"Blessed is the man that feareth the Lord, that delighteth greatly in his commandments.... Surely he shall not be moved for ever: the righteous shall be in everlasting remembrance. He shall not be afraid of evil tidings: his heart is fixed, trusting in the Lord. *His heart is established....*"

Psalm 112:1-8

Get a Heart Fix—Establish It Firmly on God's Word

FOCUS: "His heart is fixed, trusting in the Lord. His heart is established..." (Psalm 112:7-8)

Many people believe the Word with their minds, but their hearts are not necessarily *established* in it. In order to receive what God has said in His Word, it takes a revelation concerning that Word. It takes becoming established—rooted and grounded—in the Word to the place where feelings, what other people say, or what the devil can do will not move you. It takes making the decision to say, "I'm not moved by what I see. I'm not moved by what I feel. I'm only moved by the Word of God."

God exalted His Word above His Name. He put it first place above all else. To live and operate like God does, put the Word first place in your life.

Jesus and the Word agree because they are one (John 1:1-2, 14). Jesus always points man to the Word. "If ye continue in my word, then are ye my disciples indeed" (John 8:31). "If ye abide in me, and my words abide in you, ye shall ask what ye will, and it shall be done unto you" (John 15:7). To make Jesus Lord is to make the Word final authority.

If a believer wants God to get involved in all that he is doing, he must do what God's Word says to do.

Most believers do not have a faith problem. They have a Word problem. The God kind of faith was received at the time of the new birth. Faith is one of the forces that make up the fruit of the re-created human spirit. However, the mind was not re-created. So it must be renewed. This is why believers can have a Word problem. Until their mind is renewed

> *To make Jesus Lord is to make the Word final authority.*

by the Word of God, they cannot be established in His will.

For example, a believer may know what the Word says about healing but not be established in "by His stripes ye were healed." His words, "I know I'm healed, *but...*" are immediately followed by a statement of unbelief. His heart is not established in the area of healing.

A man with an established heart is unwavering, never doubting. His heart is fixed. He's not leaning to his own understanding; he's trusting in the Lord (Proverbs 3:5). He stands in the awareness that if God is for him, no one can successfully be his enemy. It is not necessary for him to stop and think about it—he knows that. He says, "All things are possible to me because I am a believer." Then he takes the next step and finds out what the Word says and acts on it. In order to trust in the Lord, he has to trust in His Word.

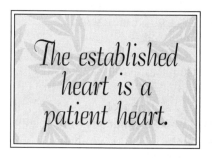

The established heart is a patient heart.

The established heart is a patient heart. It is one who, after having done the will of God, will patiently stand on the Word until it receives the promise. Hebrews 10:35-36 says, "Cast not away therefore your confidence, which hath great recompence of reward. For ye have need of patience, that, after ye have done the will of God, ye might receive the promise." The established heart will not relent or turn back but is constant—the same yesterday, today and forever. ༺ༀ༻

Everyone's heart is established on something—the Word of God or the world's system of operation. The world's way is fear, sickness, poverty, weakness and death. But God's way is faith and life. If you don't fill yourself with the Word, you can become established in the negative things that are all around you.

Now Begin Enjoying It

So make a decision to feed on the Word continually. Become established in it. God told Joshua to meditate in the Word *day and night,* and then he would be prosperous and have good success (Joshua 1:8). That is still true today.

The world's way is temporal and subject to change. But the Word works—one hundred percent of the time.

CD 11 Outlined

I. The believer whose heart is established on the Word is trusting in the Lord and believes the Word, regardless of circumstances
    A. The things of God and the power of God can work in his life
    B. Becoming established takes a revelation of the Word
    C. John 8:31

II. The God kind of faith was received at the new birth as part of the re-created human spirit
    A. The mind was not re-created. It must be renewed
    B. The mind must be renewed to the Word of God to become established in His will

III. The Word-ruled mind is never prepared to fail (James 1:5-8)
    A. It is a mind that doesn't waver
    B. It is a mind dominated by God's thoughts, nature and ways
    C. We have the mind of Christ (1 Corinthians 2:16)
    D. You are ruled by one or the other—ordinary impulses or God's Word
        1. Faith or fear
        2. Sickness or health
        3. Poverty or abundance
        4. Power or weakness

IV. The faith confession
    A. Brings glory to the Father
    B. Brings joy to Jesus
    C. Brings victory to your own heart

V. The established heart is one that meditates upon God's Word
    A. He delights greatly in God's commandments
    B. Meditating the Word brings success (Joshua 1:8)

Study Questions

(1) Why does making Jesus Lord make the Word final authority? _____

_____

_____

_____

(2) What is one of the major problems among believers today? _____

_____

_____

_____

(3) Explain the difference between head knowledge and the established

heart. _____

_____

_____

_____

_____

(4) Why is a person who is rooted and grounded in the Word

successful? _____

_____

_____

_____

(5) List some attributes of a person with an established heart. _____

_____

_____

_____

Study Notes

"For with the heart man
believeth unto righteousness;
and with the mouth
confession is made unto
salvation."

Romans 10:10

Put your faith into action...
start believing with your heart instead of your head...
and bring the power of God on the scene.

CD TWELVE
Believing With the Heart

There Is a Difference Between Believing With the Heart and Believing With the Head

"*F*or we walk by faith, not by sight."

2 Corinthians 5:7

Believing With the Heart Takes Revelation Knowledge

FOCUS: "Afterward he appeared unto the eleven as they sat at meat, and upbraided them with their unbelief and hardness of heart, because they believed not them which had seen him after he was risen" (Mark 16:14).

In this study, we're going to talk about believing with the heart, not the head.

In Mark 16:14, we see that Jesus spoke to His disciples concerning their unbelief and hardheartedness because they did not believe the testimony of those who had seen Him after His resurrection.

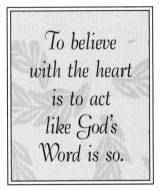

To believe with the heart is to act like God's Word is so.

We get the idea that a hardhearted person is someone who is mean and gruff. But notice who Jesus called hardhearted. The Word of God says it's a person who refuses to believe when someone tells them the Word of God, or someone who *refuses* to believe a testimony. Basically, unbelief itself is believing something other than what God has said.

After being told by the other disciples that Jesus had risen from the dead, Thomas would not accept what they said until he saw Jesus for himself. Jesus instructed him to "be not faithless, but believing" (John 20:27).

You can mentally assent to something being true but never believe it with your heart. Believing is an action word. When you begin to believe the Word is true, you will act on it, by faith. To believe with the heart is to act like God's Word is so. It is operating the Word that has been revealed to your spirit by the Holy Spirit.

In a pressure situation, you will quickly find out if the knowledge you are operating in is sense knowledge or revelation knowledge. What you do under pressure reveals what you believe, not just what you think you believe. You'll find out where your faith is. Make sure that the Word in your spirit is activated in faith. Act like the Word that has been revealed to you is true.

When you act according to what the Word says, you are not a hearer only but a doer of that Word. As you feed on God's Word, the faith that resides in your spirit will develop and grow until you would not think of acting any other way.

Believing with the heart is man's responsibility. God gave you His faith for your very own, but He will not do your believing for you. He functions by faith and you must function by faith. Trust in Him with all your heart and lean not to your own understanding (Proverbs 3:5).

How do you trust God with your heart? By getting to know Him on a personal basis through fellowship in His Word. Put God's Word first place and feed it into your heart. Receive the written Word as God speaking to you personally about what He will do for you NOW! ∞

Do not consider natural, physical evidence as what you believe. Remember, we walk by faith, not by sight (2 Corinthians 5:7). Choose to believe the Word instead. Faith in God's Word is the answer to every need in life. Consider Jesus, not your problems.

Form an image of the Word on the inside of you. Allow that inner image to grow to the point where it is more real to you than what you can see in the natural. See yourself succeed. Believe who you are in Christ. All things are possible to you as a believer (Mark 9:23).

The Word in you bears the fruit (Colossians 1:5-6). The Word goes into your spirit and faith comes out, putting the supernatural power of

God into operation—changing things in the natural, physical world into the desired result. The manifestation is the fruit of the Word from the inner man. "If ye abide in me, and my words abide in you, ye shall ask what ye will, and it shall be done unto you. Herein is my Father glorified, that ye bear much fruit; so shall ye be my disciples" (John 15:7-8).

Now Begin Enjoying It

We do not lack for anything. Jesus has already provided all our needs met (Philippians 4:19). We just need to develop the Word in us.

So become skillful in handling the Word. Get over on your faith—that's where the power is. Start believing with your heart instead of your head.

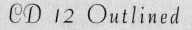 # CD 12 Outlined

I. Unbelief is refusing to believe what God has said

II. Believe with the heart, not the head
   A. You will find out where your faith is in pressure situations
   B. Believing is our responsibility
   C. Lean not to your own understanding (Proverbs 3:5)
   D. We walk by faith, not by sight (2 Corinthians 5:7)

III. How do you trust God with your heart?
   A. Put God and His Word first place
   B. Do not consider the physical realm—faith in the Word is the answer
   C. Consider Jesus—not the problem

IV. Form an inner image with the Word
   A. See yourself successful
   B. Believe who you are in Christ
   C. You can do all things through Christ (Philippians 4:13)
   D. All things are possible to the believer (Mark 9:23)

V. Manifestation is the fruit of the Word in the inner man

VI. You do not lack anything
   A. Jesus has provided all your needs (Philippians 4:19)
   B. You just need to develop the Word in you—become skillful in the word of righteousness (Hebrews 5:13)
   C. Let your spirit be in ascendancy over the flesh

Study Questions

(1) Define unbelief. _____

_____

_____

_____

(2) Explain the difference between believing with the heart and mental assent. _____

_____

_____

_____

(3) How do you trust God with your heart?_____

_____

_____

_____

_____

(4) Why is it necessary for the inner image of yourself to be in accordance with the Word? _____

_____

_____

_____

(5) How does the Word in you bear fruit? _____

_____

_____

_____

_____

Study Notes

"Trust in the Lord with all thine heart; and lean not unto thine own understanding."
Proverbs 3:5

Prayer for Salvation and Baptism in the Holy Spirit

Heavenly Father, I come to You in the Name of Jesus. Your Word says, "Whosoever shall call on the name of the Lord shall be saved" (Acts 2:21). I am calling on You. I pray and ask Jesus to come into my heart and be Lord over my life according to Romans 10:9-10: "If thou shalt confess with thy mouth the Lord Jesus, and shalt believe in thine heart that God hath raised him from the dead, thou shalt be saved. For with the heart man believeth unto righteousness; and with the mouth confession is made unto salvation." I do that now. I confess that Jesus is Lord, and I believe in my heart that God raised Him from the dead.

I am now reborn! I am a Christian—a child of Almighty God! I am saved! You also said in Your Word, "If ye then, being evil, know how to give good gifts unto your children: HOW MUCH MORE shall your heavenly Father give the Holy Spirit to them that ask him?" (Luke 11:13). I'm also asking You to fill me with the Holy Spirit. Holy Spirit, rise up within me as I praise God. I fully expect to speak with other tongues as You give me the utterance (Acts 2:4). In Jesus' Name. Amen!

Begin to praise God for filling you with the Holy Spirit. Speak those words and syllables you receive—not in your own language, but the language given to you by the Holy Spirit. You have to use your own voice. God will not force you to speak. Don't be concerned with how it sounds. It is a heavenly language!

Continue with the blessing God has given you and pray in the spirit every day.

You are a born-again, Spirit-filled believer. You'll never be the same!

Find a good church that boldly preaches God's Word and obeys it. Become part of a church family who will love and care for you as you love and care for them.

We need to be connected to each other. It increases our strength in God. It's God's plan for us.

Make it a habit to watch the *Believer's Voice of Victory* television broadcast and become a doer of the Word, who is blessed in his doing (James 1:22-25).

About the Author

Kenneth Copeland is co-founder and president of Kenneth Copeland Ministries in Fort Worth, Texas, and best-selling author of books that include *How to Discipline Your Flesh* and *Honor—Walking in Honesty, Truth and Integrity.*

Since 1967, Kenneth has been a minister of the gospel of Christ and teacher of God's Word. He is also the artist on award-winning albums such as his Grammy-nominated *Only the Redeemed, In His Presence, He Is Jehovah, Just a Closer Walk* and *Big Band Gospel.* He also co-stars as the character Wichita Slim in the children's adventure videos *The Gunslinger, Covenant Rider* and the movie *The Treasure of Eagle Mountain,* and as Daniel Lyon in the Commander Kellie and the Superkids_{TM} videos *Armor of Light* and *Judgment: The Trial of Commander Kellie.* Kenneth also co-stars as a Hispanic godfather in the 2009 movie *The Rally.*

With the help of offices and staff in the United States, Canada, England, Australia, South Africa, Ukraine and Singapore, Kenneth is fulfilling his vision to boldly preach the uncompromised WORD of God from the top of this world, to the bottom, and all the way around. His ministry reaches millions of people worldwide through daily and Sunday TV broadcasts, magazines, teaching audios and videos, conventions and campaigns, and the World Wide Web.

Learn more about Kenneth Copeland Ministries
by visiting our website at **kcm.org**

When The LORD first spoke to Kenneth and Gloria Copeland about starting the *Believer's Voice of Victory* magazine...

He said: *This is your seed. Give it to everyone who ever responds to your ministry, and don't ever allow anyone to pay for a subscription!*

For more than 40 years, it has been the joy of Kenneth Copeland Ministries to bring the good news to believers. Readers enjoy teaching from ministers who write from lives of living contact with God, and testimonies from believers experiencing victory through God's WORD in their everyday lives.

Today, the *BVOV* magazine is mailed monthly, bringing encouragement and blessing to believers around the world. Many even use it as a ministry tool, passing it on to others who desire to know Jesus and grow in their faith!

Request your FREE subscription to the
***Believer's Voice of Victory* magazine today!**

Go to **freevictory.com** to subscribe online, or call us at
1-800-600-7395 (U.S. only) or **+1-817-852-6000**.

We're Here for You!®

Your growth in God's WORD and victory in Jesus are at the very center of our hearts. In every way God has equipped us, we will help you deal with the issues facing you, so you can be the **victorious overcomer** He has planned for you to be.

The mission of Kenneth Copeland Ministries is about all of us growing and going together. Our prayer is that you will take full advantage of all The LORD has given us to share with you.

Wherever you are in the world, you can watch the *Believer's Voice of Victory* broadcast on television (check your local listings), the Internet at kcm.org or on our digital Roku channel.

Our website, **kcm.org,** gives you access to every resource we've developed for your victory. And, you can find contact information for our international offices in Africa, Asia, Australia, Canada, Europe, Ukraine and our headquarters in the United States.

Each office is staffed with devoted men and women, ready to serve and pray with you. You can contact the worldwide office nearest you for assistance, and you can call us for prayer at our U.S. number, +1-817-852-6000, 24 hours every day!

We encourage you to connect with us often and let us be part of your everyday walk of faith!

Jesus Is LORD!

Kenneth & Gloria Copeland

Kenneth and Gloria Copeland